Brooklyn Beaver Almost Builds a Dam

Written by Florenza Lee
Illustrated by Eduardo Paj

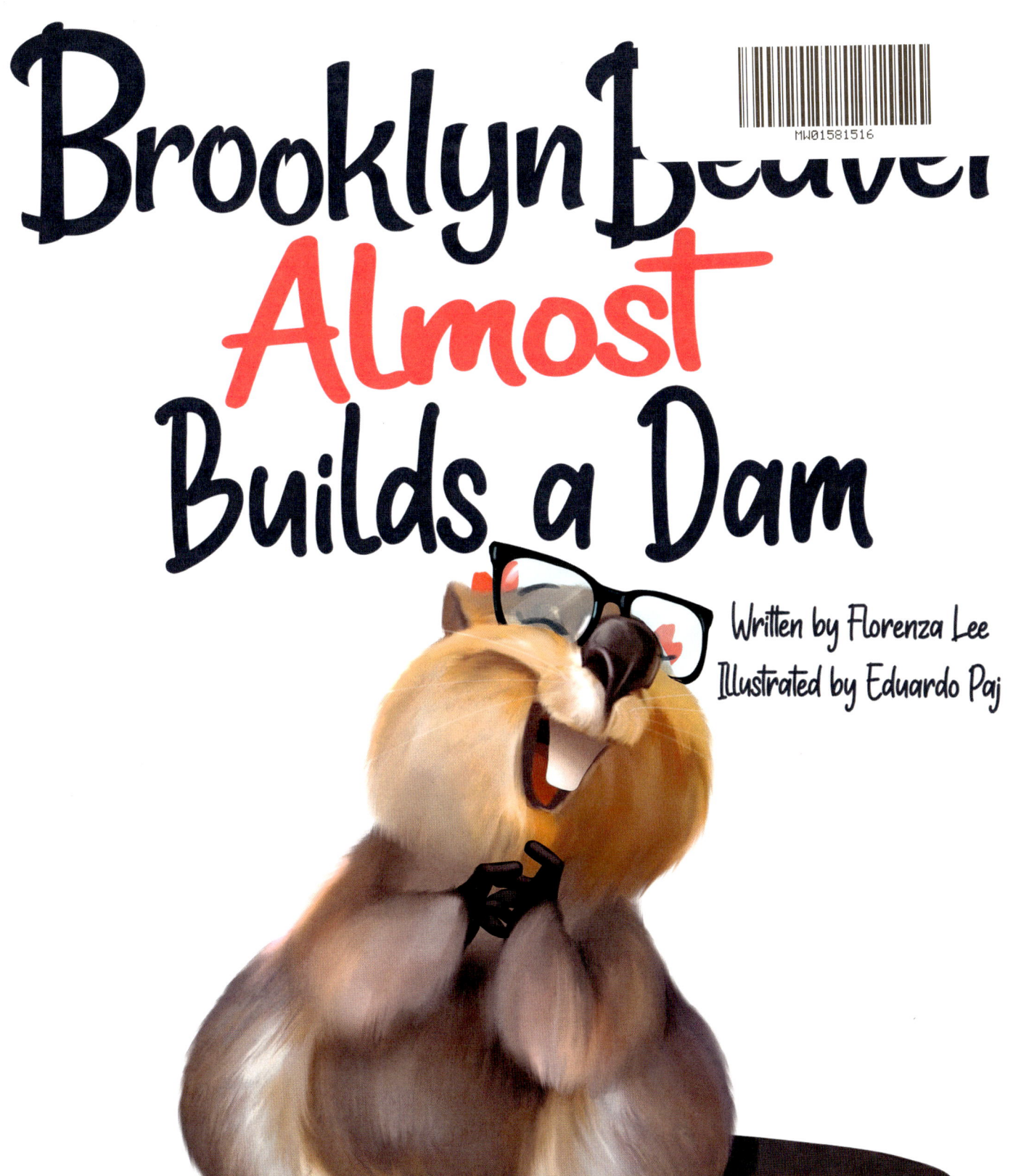

FLORENZA DENISE LEE
ILLUSTRATED BY EDUARDO PAJ

Brooklyn Beaver ALMOST Builds a Dam Text and Illustrations copyright @ 2021 by Words to Ponder Publishing Company, LLC.

Illustrated by Eduardo Paj.

First Paperback

This book is protected under the copyright laws of the United States and other countries throughout the world. Although inspired by real individuals, the story, all names, characters, and incidents portrayed are fictitious. No identification with actual persons (living or deceased), places, buildings, or products is intended or should be inferred. All rights reserved. No part of this book, or the characters within it, may be reproduced or transmitted in any form or by any mechanical means, including information storage and retrieval systems, without written permission from the publisher, Words to Ponder Publishing Company, LLC, except by reviewer, who may quote passages in a review.

Address inquiries to Contact@florenza.org

ISBN 978-1-941328-55-2

Library of Congress Number 2021912786

Words to Ponder Publishing Company, LLC

I dedicate this book to my family, Trefus, Jessica, and Missy,
for being my first and loudest cheerleaders.
And to all the parents, caregivers, educators, and children who enjoy
reading my book-babies as much as I do while creating them.
Happy reading,
Florenza

This Book Belongs To:

_____

To, Ben
Be bold!
Love,

"I must hurry," huffs Brooklyn. "I simply cannot be late! I don't know why I agreed to haul all the supplies by myself," she says while wiping sweat from her brow. "This is a task for two... make that six!"

"Good thing Bryceson and I previously chomped down the logs, or we'd be up a creek without a paddle!" Brooklyn pauses and chuckles at the joke. "Beavers don't need boats," she giggles, "or paddles for that matter!"

"Where are you going in such a hurry?" inquires Wrenn.
"To meet Bryceson," explains Brooklyn.
"What if I assist you?" she offers.
Brooklyn is curious. "How? You're not strong enough to push the barrow."

"True. But I can use these for my nest," states Wrenn.
"A lighter load will help you get there quicker!"
Brooklyn agrees that a few sticks will not hinder
her build and may help her to arrive faster.
"Thank you kindly, my friend. Happy building!"
And off Wrenn flies.

"That helped some, but not much," says
Brooklyn realizing she still had
a long journey ahead.
"Excuse me," comes a squeak.
"Where are you going in such a tizzy?"
"Who said that?" Brooklyn squints
as she turns her head from side to side.
"I did. Look down here!"
"And who are you?" inquires Brooklyn,
glancing downward.

"My name is Giovanna. Might I assist you in your journey?"
"How?" asks Brooklyn. "You are so tiny."
"By taking a few of these. They do look delicious!"
Wings flapping, she begins to munch on a handful of leaves.
"Bon appetite," replies Brooklyn as she continues on her journey.
"Gratitude and happy building." Off she happily hops.

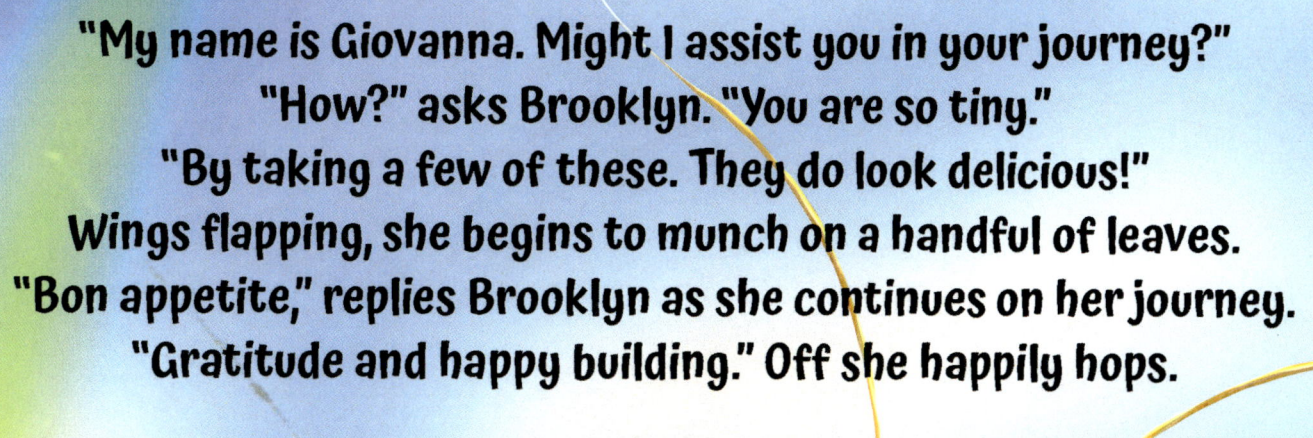

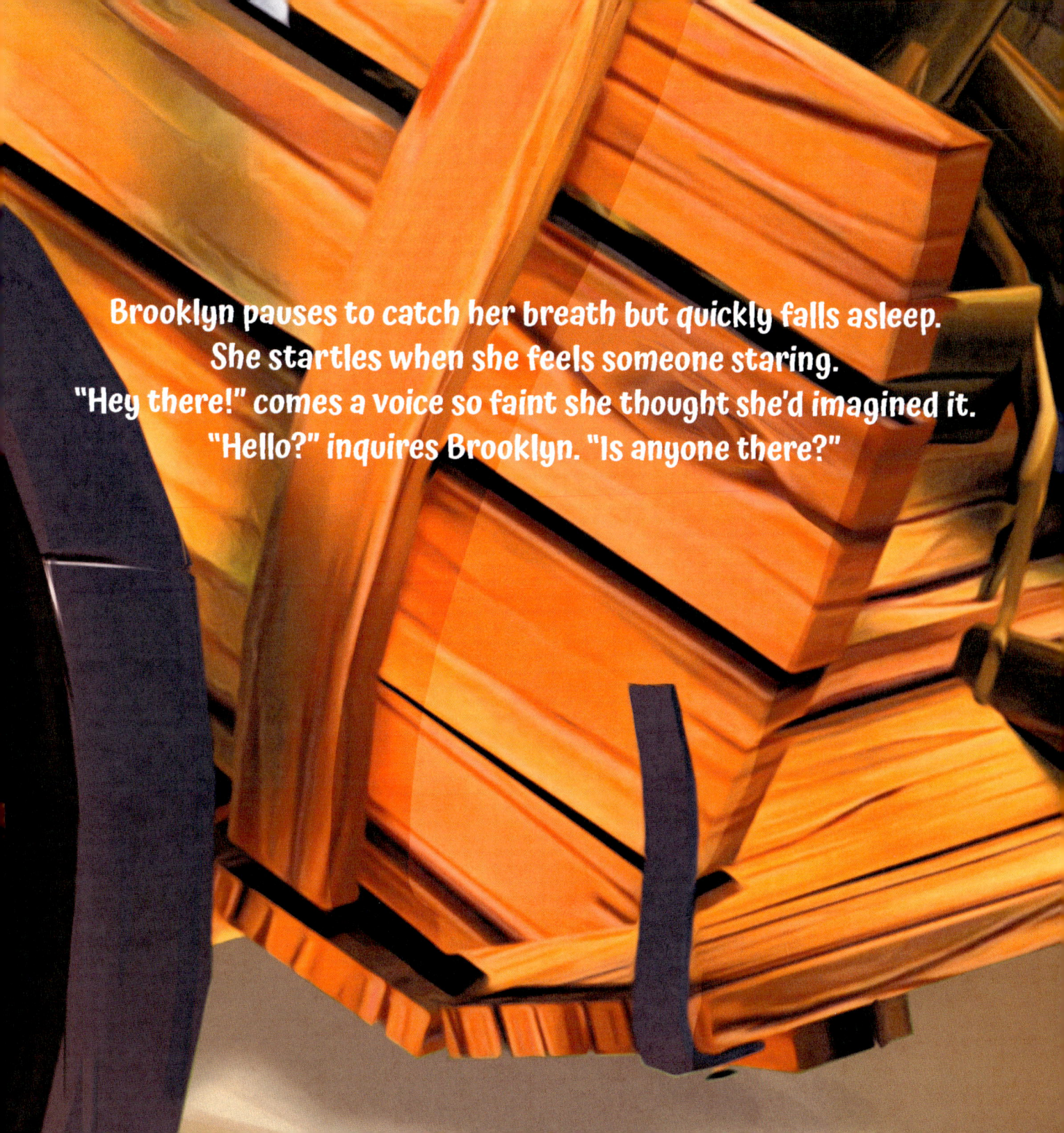

Brooklyn pauses to catch her breath but quickly falls asleep.
She startles when she feels someone staring.
"Hey there!" comes a voice so faint she thought she'd imagined it.
"Hello?" inquires Brooklyn. "Is anyone there?"

"Over here. I'm sorry to interrupt your nap. I'm Rae. I could really use a few stones to cover the opening to my burrow."
She inspects the rocks inside Brooklyn's barrow.
"I don't see why not," says Brooklyn. "It may ease the task so I can continue on my journey."
Quickly pawing several stones, Rae hops away and then returns for more. "I appreciate this. Have fun building," she shouts over her shoulder!

"Finally," pants Brooklyn. "I'm here!"
"It's about time. What took you so long?" scolds her older brother. "Let's hurry before it's too dark to…"
Looking into the barrow, Bryceson is flabbergasted.

"Is this all that you've gathered?" he bellows.
"You could have carried these scraps in your paws."
As he yells, Brooklyn peers into the barrow.
She too, could not believe her eyes.

Brooklyn gazes downward as she kicks a pebble. "Not exactly," she whispers. But, before she could say anything else, Bryceson storms away, flapping his arms and shaking his head.

"What am I going to do now?" After a few moments, Brooklyn stands and shouts, "Ah-ha!" She then retrieves her wheelbarrow and quickly trots away. Retracing her steps, she arrives at Rae's burrow.

Knock! Knock! "Is anyone home?" calls Brooklyn.
"Oh, hello. How may I help you?" asks Rae.
"I didn't realize how important the stones are to my task of building a dam," says Brooklyn in a timid voice.
"I must ask you to give them back, please."

"Oh, Dear," says Rae. "I have already used them."
Tears sting Brooklyn's eyes.
"But I must have them," she pleads.
"I cannot give you the exact ones," says Rae.
"But will these work? They were too large for
me to use." She shows Brooklyn
a massive pile of rocks.
"These are perfect. Thank you very much,"
says Brooklyn as she continues on her journey.

Ding dong chimes the doorbell. "I need to have my leaves back," Brooklyn says as soon as the door opens. "I wish I could return them, but I have already eaten them all," Giovanna says while scratching her tummy. "And they were delicious."
"Oh, my goodness," cries Brooklyn.
"Wait, I have a bale of hay. Will that work instead?" She then ushers Brooklyn out back.
"This is perfect. Thank you so much!"
They add it to the other items in the barrow, and off they go.

"Hello up there," shouts Brooklyn.
"How may I help you?"
comes the response.
"I'd like to ask for my twigs back, please."
"May I ask why are you requesting to have them back?"
Brooklyn nods and says,
"I didn't realize how important they are to build the dam."

"I'm sorry, but I have already used them." Wrenn says as she flaps her wings. "My eggs are nestled safely inside. But I do have a pile of logs in the back," announces Wrenn. "They are far too large for my use. You are free to have those." Brooklyn and the others quickly race to the back. "These are perfect," shouts Brooklyn as they pile them into the barrow.

Returning with her treasure trove, "I hope I'm not too late,"
Brooklyn pants. "I got back as soon as I could."
Bryceson rubs his eyes in disbelief.
The barrow is completely full.
"And she brought help," chime all the animals.
"Brooklyn was so generous to us;
we wanted to return the favor. We're here to assist."
"This is amazing," replies Bryceson, as he gives his sister a hug.

The animals assisted with constructing the dam, then all sit down to enjoy a delicious meal. Embracing her brother, Brooklyn says, "Next year, you'll gather the supplies, and I'll wait by the river's edge."

With a huge grin, the animals reply, "How about we do it together?"

ABOUT THE AUTHOR

Florenza is an author, publisher, narrative coach, speaker, radio talk show host, Master Storyteller, Advocate, wife, and mother.

Florenza and her husband, CSM (Ret US Army) Trefus Lee, have been married for nearly 38 years and reside in Chagrin Falls, Ohio.

Their daughters, Jessica and Missy, call Las Vegas, NV, and Chagrin Falls, Ohio, home.

Please follow and engage virtually with Florenza via the following links.

Instagram: https://bit.ly/InstagramPagefld
Amazon Author: https://bit.ly/amazonauthorpagefdl
Kutafakari Bookstore: https://bit.ly/KutafakariBookstore
Facebook: https://www.facebook.com/Florenza.Denise.Lee/
Website: https://bit.ly/websitefdl
Mailing List https://bit.ly/StayInTheFlo
Pinterest http://bit.ly/PinterestFlo
BookBub: https://bit.ly/LeeFBookbub
GoodReads: https://bit.ly/LeeFGoodreads

Published titles by Florenza are:

Adventurous Olivia's Alphabet Quest
Adventurous Olivia's Calm Quest- A Book on Mindfulness
Amiri's Birthday Wish
Barry Bear's Very Best, Learning to Say No to Negative Influences
If…The Story of Faith Walker
Manny & Tutu
Mind Your Manners Mia
There's No Place Like My Own Home
This Time Next Year
The Tail of Max the Mindless Dog, A Children's Book on Mindfulness
Welcome Home Daddy, Love Lexi
When Life Gives Us Wind

Learn more by visiting her website,
www.florenza.org.

Made in the USA
Monee, IL
16 October 2021

79562712R00029